BEYOND BASICS
ACOUSTIC SLIDE GUITAR

KEITH WYATT

8.96

Editor: Aaron Stang
Additional Text and Music Examples: Hemme Luttjeboer
Artist Photography courtesy of Ebet Roberts
Slide Photography Courtesy of Shelly Lutgen and the BigHeart Slide Co.
Art Design: Joseph Klucar

WARNER BROS. PUBLICATIONS
Warner Music Group
An AOL Time Warner Company
USA: 15800 NW 48th Avenue, Miami, FL 33014

WARNER/CHAPPELL MUSIC

CANADA: 15800 N.W. 48th AVENUE
MIAMI, FLORIDA 33014
SCANDINAVIA: P.O. BOX 533, VENDEVAGEN 85 B
S-182 15, DANDERYD, SWEDEN
AUSTRALIA: P.O. BOX 353
3 TALAVERA ROAD, NORTH RYDE N.S.W. 2113
ASIA: THE PENINSULA OFFICE TOWER, 12th FLOOR
18 MIDDLE ROAD
TSIM SHA TSUI, KOWLOON, HONG KONG

NUOVA CARISCH

ITALY: VIA CAMPANIA, 12
20098 S. GIULIANO MILANESE (MI)
ZONA INDUSTRIALE SESTO ULTERIANO
SPAIN: MAGALLANES, 25
28015 MADRID
FRANCE: CARISCH MUSICOM,
25, RUE D'HAUTEVILLE, 75010 PARIS

INTERNATIONAL MUSIC PUBLICATIONS LIMITED

ENGLAND: GRIFFIN HOUSE,
161 HAMMERSMITH ROAD, LONDON W6 8BS
GERMANY: MARSTALLSTR. 8, D-80539 MUNCHEN
DENMARK: DANMUSIK, VOGNMAGERGADE 7
DK 1120 KOBENHAVNK

CONTENTS

CD
(2)

INTRODUCTION

Welcome to *Acoustic Slide Guitar.* This book will guide you through the long and varied history and technique of playing acoustic slide guitar. The acoustic slide guitar has an ambiguous beginning that dates back to when the state of Hawaii became a U.S. territory and its popularity was bolstered by a Hawaiian music craze around the turn of the century. A major feature of Hawaiian music is the sound of the slide guitar. At the same time, musicians in the Mississippi Delta were molding their own technique on the guitar and were influenced by the Hawaiian trend. A "down home" sound materialized and it is the source of that sound that is the subject of this book.

ABOUT THE BOOK

In this book we'll examine types of slides, left and right hand techniques, open tunings, phrasing, vibrato and intonation. The styles of "Muddy Waters" and "Elmore James" are featured with examples in tablature as well as standard notation to accommodate reading in open tunings. You can follow each example with the accompanying CD, which allows you to fully scrutinize and repeat each topic and technique as needed. Play and repeat as often as you wish. Enjoy!

SECTION 1:
TYPES OF SLIDES

The first subject to be addressed with slide guitar playing is the slide itself. Over the years everything and anything conceivable to make a sound on a string was used as a slide. Primitive appendages such as a bone or a knife were used as opposed to today's more sophisticated glass or metal slides.

Specialized slide guitars with a "Hawaiian" ancestry include the "Dobro," or resonator guitar, which utilizes a metal resonator on the top that amplifies the sound. A variation of this guitar is the "National Steel" guitar — made completely out of steel and *extremely* loud. But for that "down home" sound a standard steel string acoustic guitar is best.

The acoustic guitar in general is well suited for slide because the strings and action are almost natural requisites in duplicating the "slide sound." The strings should be fairly heavy and the action (the distance between the strings and the neck itself) should be a little off the frets so that when you play a note with the slide you don't hear any fret buzz.

Glass slides are inexpensive and are often made from a type of medical or surgical glass. Earlier glass slides were homemade and created from the tops of wine bottles. An option would be the big heavy brass slide but the most popular is the glass slide. The main difference with glass slides is the thickness of the glass itself. For a big fat sound use the thick heavier slide. They also come in different diameters depending on which finger you prefer to use the slide. For purposes of demonstration in this book, place the slide on the 4th finger of your left hand. The slide should fit rather snugly up to the first knuckle and you should be able to bend the finger as well. Try different types and experiment but you should stick with one kind and feel comfortable with the slide you use.

RORY BLOCK

CD 5

SECTION 2: LEFT AND RIGHT HAND TECHNIQUES

There is a definite technique to playing the slide that involves a combination of both hands together. With the slide on the 4th finger of your left hand place it on the neck so that it is parallel to the frets. The remaining 3 fingers should follow behind the slide with the index finger barely resting on the strings, not pressing down. All the motion in the slide comes from the wrist and the arm with the index finger as a guide. This finger also helps to "dampen" unwanted sounds.

CD 6

Example 1

In order to play a note exactly in tune place the slide directly over the fret. Normally to produce a note you place a finger between two frets. When playing slide guitar the slide sits *directly* above the 9th fret (E). It will take practice to play slide in tune because you are actually playing "one finger fretless guitar." The frets are only there to guide you. In effect the slide becomes a moving fret.

(Note: Most of the examples in this book are written in 4/4 with a shuffle feel ♩♩ = ♩♪ .)

CD 7

Example 2a

The left hand controls the choice of notes, coupled with good intonation, but the right hand controls the sound of the notes. As in standard guitar playing there are different right hand approaches. One way is to play without a pick and just use bare thumb and fingers as in this example.

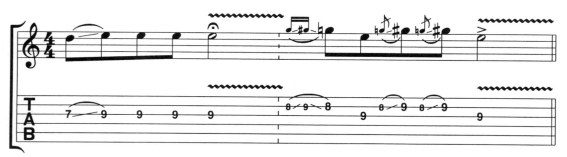

CD ⑧

Example 2b

This example demonstrates the typical flat pick approach. The two different styles are distinct, with the flat pick being the louder and more likely to exude unwanted sounds. (A technique called "damping" is used to eliminate unwanted notes and emphasize intended notes.)

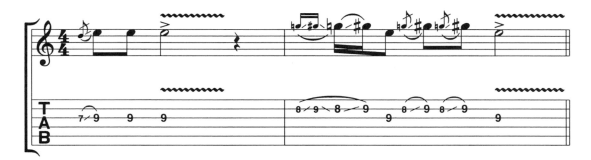

CD ⑨

Example 3

Another right hand option for acoustic slide playing is the **thumb pick.** It provides a facile combination of pick and fingers. The thumb plays clear bass notes and allows all the fingers to play freely and dampen the remaining strings. In this example use the thumb pick to play the steady 8th notes on the 6th string. You can also use the thumb pick as a flat pick as demonstrated in the last measure.

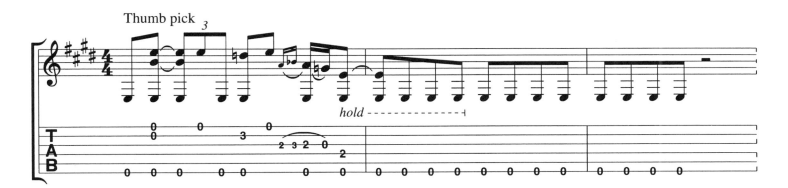

Example 4a: Damping

Damping is the essence of the "slide sound." The importance of this technique is demonstrated here in the key of E major. In standard tuning the best position for slide guitar in this key is around the 9th fret. The E major triad is conveniently grouped across three strings at the 9th fret so with the one finger slide approach you can play this maximum number of notes.

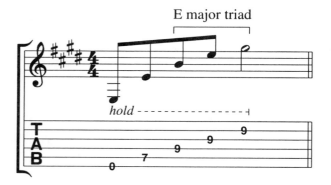

Example 4b

This is a two measure phrase without the "damping" technique. Notice how the notes ring into one another.

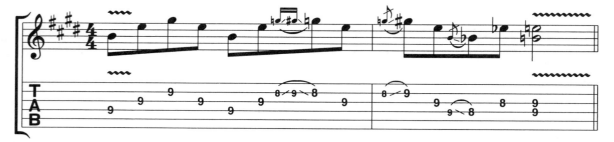

Example 5a

This single measure demonstrates the "damping" technique in detail. In order to execute it properly, hold the flat pick between the thumb and forefinger and strike the 4th string "E" at the 9th fret. The remaining three fingers simply rest on the 1st, 2nd and 3rd strings and the thumb touches the 5th string. By isolating the 4th string it should be the only note that rings when you strike it. In order to "damp" it, immediately place your thumb back on the string.

CD
(13) *Example 5b*

Here are four measures of subtle damping on the 2nd, 3rd and 4th strings. Listen carefully to the eighth note "E" arpeggio. It should have a slight staccato effect.

CD
(14) *Example 5c*

Here the "damping" technique is very effective. As soon as you strike the 3rd string, "damp" the 2nd string with the 2nd finger.

CD
(15) # Example 5d

If you play without a pick you actually have an advantage over "pick" players because of individual finger manipulation. Play this example and listen to the difference in tone. The result is a warmer and quieter sound and you have more control.

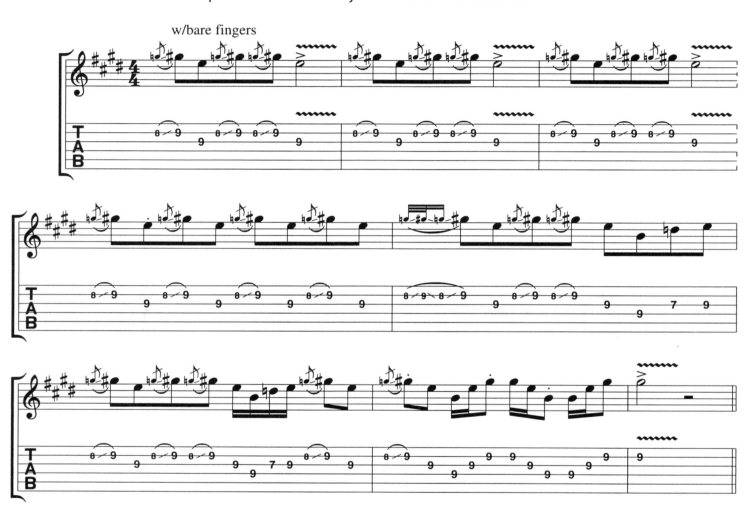

CD
(16) # Example 6

A good way to develop a good solid damping technique is to play "bugle calls." Bugle calls are derived from the notes in a triad. The E major triad in this example is a fine source for practice because most of the notes sit under the slide and you can concentrate on the right hand.

KEB' MO'

CD
(17)

SECTION 3:
DROP D & OPEN G TUNINGS

One of the most important trademark aspects of slide guitar is the sound of "open tunings." Open tunings are very beneficial to the solo acoustic slide guitarist in maintaining a rhythmic pulse and allowing consonant sounding chords to be executed with a straight barre. Unlike standard tuning, open tuning yields consonant sounds from open strings even when trying to "damp" or when you strike a wrong note. This is because each string is tuned in relation to a common chord or sound.

CD
(18) *Example 7a*

This first tuning is called the **"Drop D"** tuning. It is a partial open tuning because only the 1st string is lowered a whole step to **D**. This example gives us the actual key or chord; a **G** major triad.

(1)st string = D

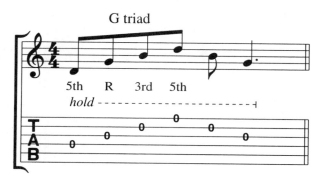

CD
(19) *Example 7b*

By returning to the "bugle calls" all the notes are now located at the 9th fret. It is much easier to play and much richer sounding. The thick sound is enhanced by the double-stops on the 1st and 2nd strings.

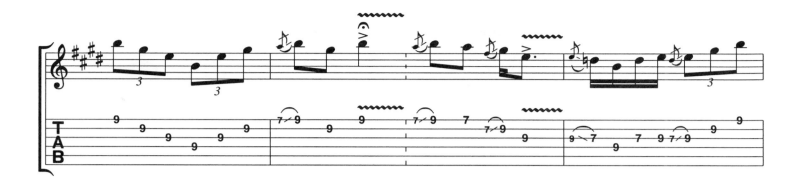

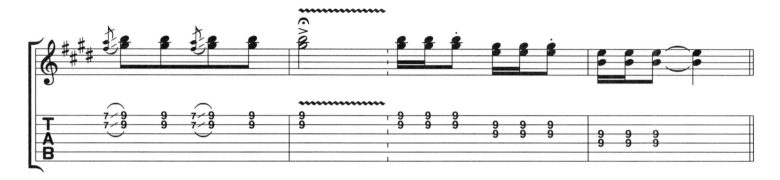

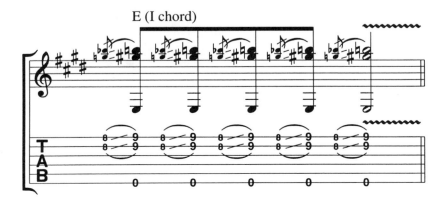

Example 8

Even though the 1st string has been lowered to D there is still no bass note that will stay in tune to the chord changes. This is an example of the problem with just a partial D tuning. There is no open "B" note as a bass for the **V** chord, B7. We can't play the same chord shape as for the "E" and "A" changes.

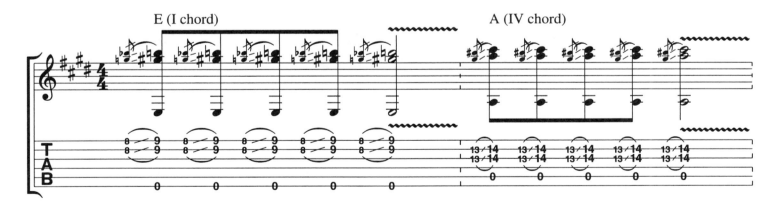

CD
(21) *Example 9a*

This is called an **"open G"** tuning. The most important thing to know about any open tuning is what the notes are in relation to the chord that you are tuned to.

↓⑥ = D ③ = G
↓⑤ = G ② = B
④ = D ↓① = D

CD
(22) *Example 9b*

Here are the roots, 3rd and 5th's of the G chord. The root "G" is on the open 5th and 3rd strings and if you want to know where you are on the neck you can use these two strings as a guide. The note C is found on the 5th string, 5th fret. The 6th, 4th and 1st strings yield the 5th (D), and the open 2nd string produces the 3rd (B). All six strings together represent a G triad with the root on the 5th and 3rd strings.

CD
(23) *Example 10*

Here is the "E" sound from a previous example. It is a full E triad at the 9th fret. Every note at this fret belongs to the E chord. So, now when you move the slide to a new fret you automatically have a bass note built in. In this case the bass note is B, the 5th of E.

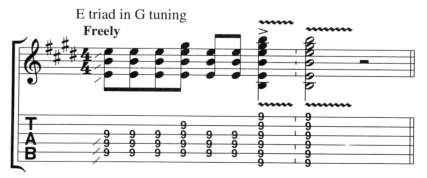

CD
(24) *Example 11*

This is a 12 bar **"Muddy Waters-Style Country Blues"** in open G tuning. The full range of bass notes, chord sounds and characteristic single note phrases are displayed and will be examined in detail in the next section.

If you have played the guitar for a while and are familiar with standard tuning the unexplored territory of an open tuning can be intimidating at first. The inherent beauty about playing in an open tuning is that it is designed to keep everything close together. You should be able to play around one fret. This is the reason for re-tuning the guitar in the first place.

MUDDY WATERS STYLE COUNTRY BLUES

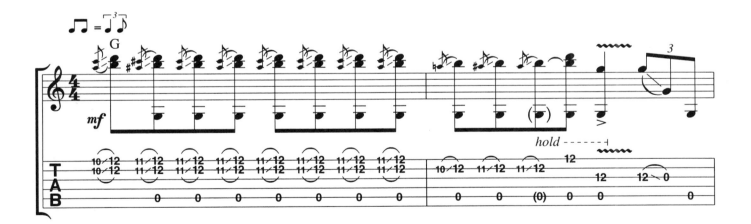

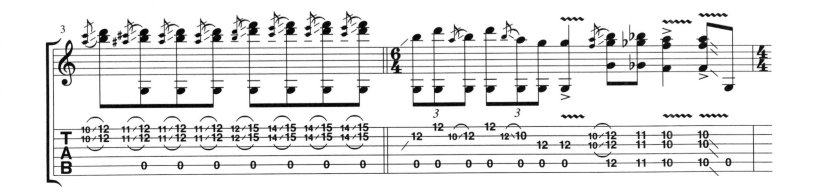

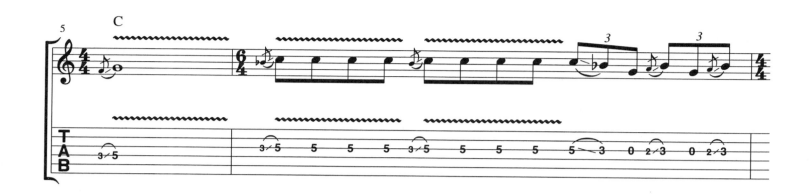

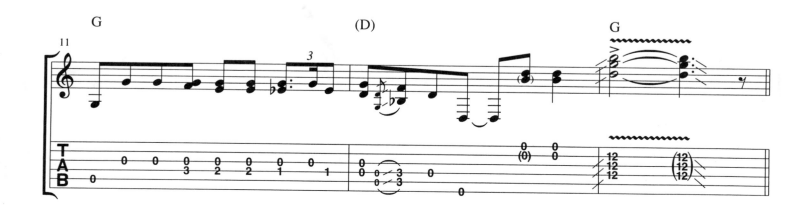

SECTION 4:
PHRASING, VIBRATO AND INTONATION

CD
25 *Example 12*

If you want to play in the key of G in open tuning, as in this example, all the notes are located at the 12th fret. To create phrases, all the notes are either at the 12th fret or within a few frets on either side. There is no need at this point to try to learn phrases or lines in the middle of the neck; it is irrelevant. All the licks you need are either at the 12th fret or in the open position.

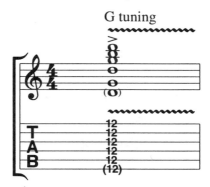

CD
26 *Example 13*

To play the standard phrases that you hear people use, whether acoustic or electric, you have to learn how to connect notes with the slide. The following ideas have as much to do with singing as they do with actual guitar playing. Because you are using a slide approach a note from a whole step away, as in this example, and slide into the intended note. You should strive for a "crying quality" in the sound. The damping technique is a very important factor here as well. The phrases tend to sound sloppy if not correctly dampened. Watch them carefully and make sure each note stands out on its own.

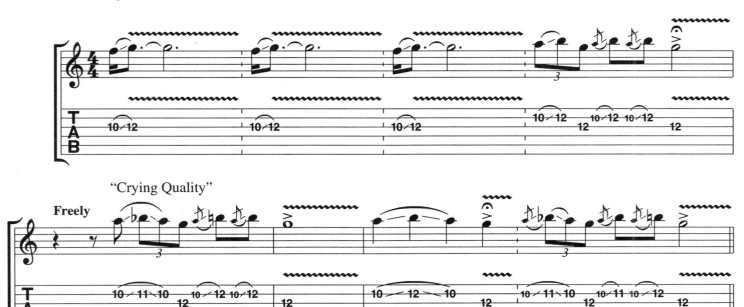

VIBRATO

Another key ingredient is **"vibrato."** It is accomplished by moving your *entire* hand from left to right. Do not separate your fingers as in standard guitar playing. The speed and width of the vibrato are personal expressions. There are some famous vibratos in the history of slide guitar. In the 1930's and '40s there was Robert Nighthawk and then came Earl Hooker in the '40s and '50s. Mick Taylor of the Rolling Stones had a distinct vibrato in the '60s. The sound of the vibrato has had a long standing tradition.

CD (27) *Example 14*

This example shows a few subtle and varied techniques of vibrato. These can range from a simple and basic style to a wide vibrato or a fast one like Muddy Waters'. Just remember to have a relaxed hand and move the intended note from side to side. Also try approaching the note from above or below.

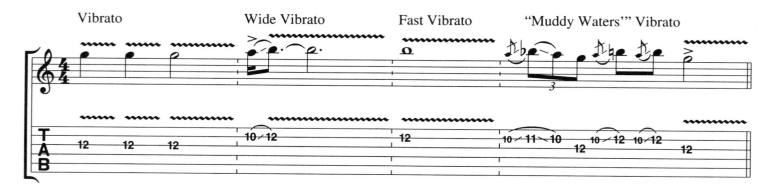

CD (28) *Example 15a*

All the notes you need to create lines or phrases are within two frets of the 12th fret as shown in this example. If you were to collect all the available notes to form a scale you would get a dominant sound — the sound of the blues. Almost all of the action takes place on the top four strings yielding this pattern.

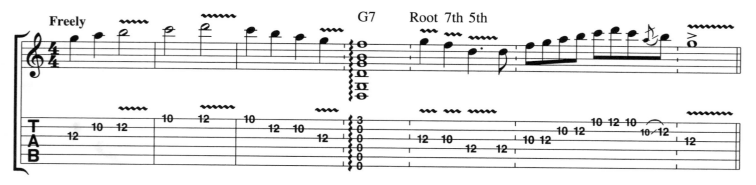

Example 15b

Here you can duplicate the 4th degree of the G7 scale, C, on the first string as well as the 2nd string.

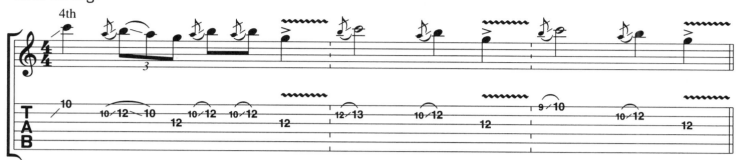

Example 16

Another valuable resource from the scale pattern is that you can play combinations of two notes. Play the double-stops with pick and finger. These are very characteristic phrases in open G tuning. If you are trying to determine a tuning from a recording listen for these types of two note phrases and shapes. These should help you figure the correct tuning whether in open G or open D.

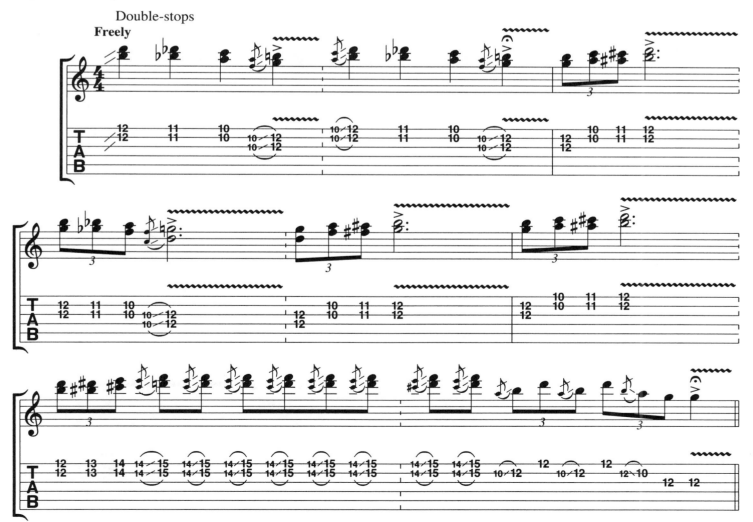

CD **31** *Example 17*

Now that you are acquainted with fundamental slide technique and with some areas in which to play, here are a few short phrases that are typical in the slide guitar vocabulary. Each phrase is one measure in length and has a beginning and an end. By linking together a series of one bar melodies you can create solos.

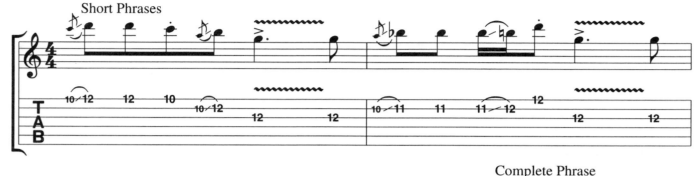

CD **32** *Example 18: Call and Response*

Here is your chance to play some of these melodic phrases. This is a play-along section of "call and response." By concentrating on the 12th position in open G you will hear a one measure phrase that is followed by a measure of rest. Simply repeat what you hear over the bar of silence. Hence the term, "call and response."

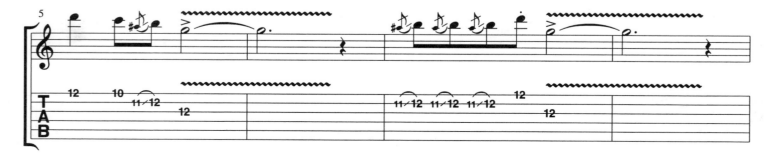

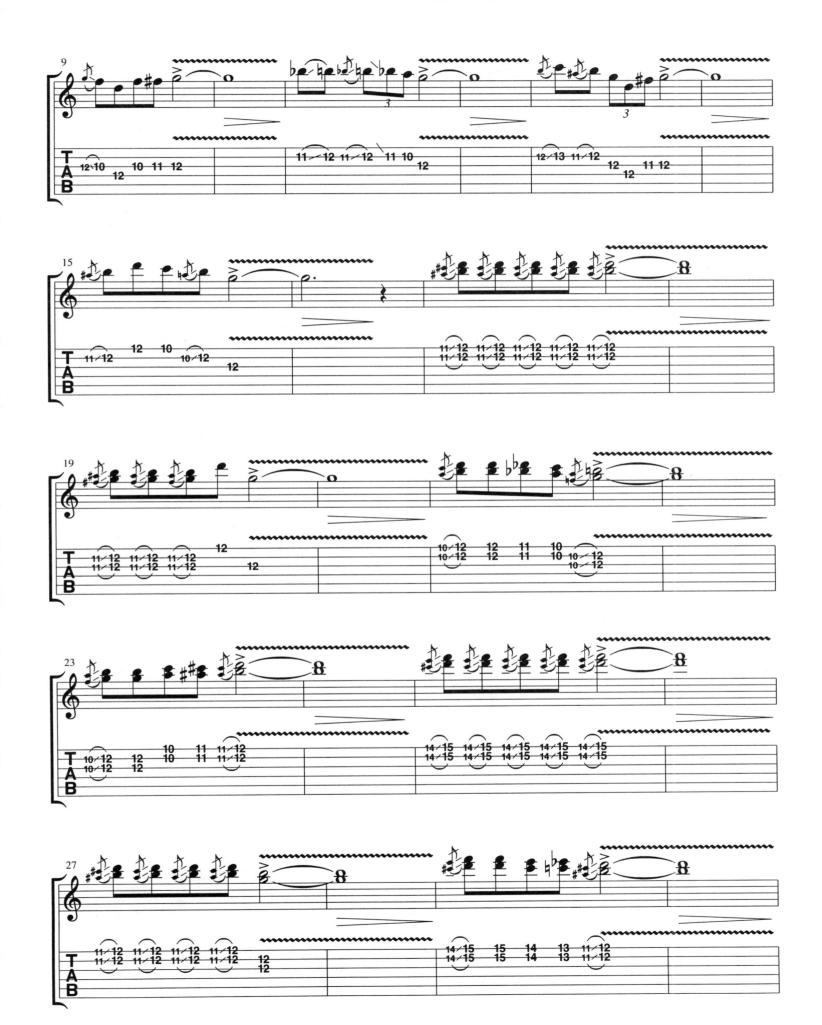

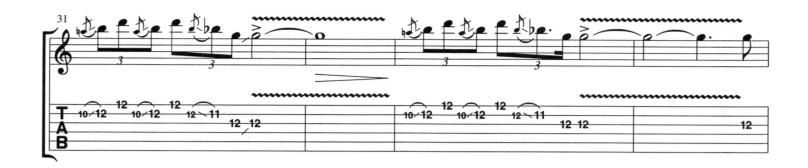

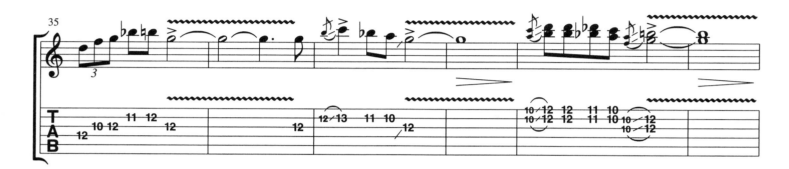

CD
(33) *Example 19*

A common sound in country blues, besides playing around the 12th in open tuning, is playing down on the low end of the guitar and using open strings. The sound of the slide rubbing against the wound strings is very characteristic of the style, giving it that "gritty" quality. The finger pattern is a consistent shape in open tuning. Sliding into each note and pulling off from the triplets is typical of a slide performance. Emphasizing beats 2 and 4 on a string below really brings across the "down home" sound. You may have seen a similar pattern in standard tuning but not with the triplets on the 5th string. This is only possible in open tuning.

CD 34

Example 20: More Call and Response

This example is similar to example 18. However, this time focus on the low end of the guitar. Listen to the phrase and then repeat it.

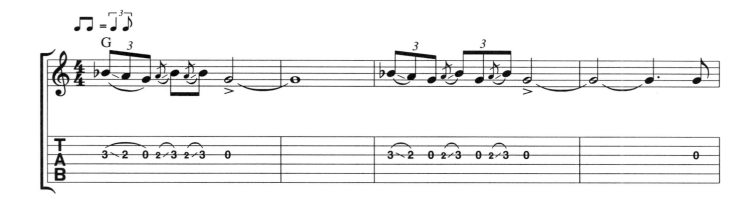

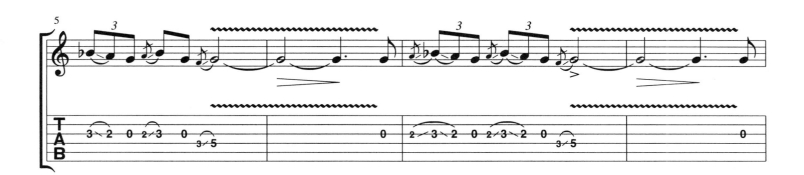

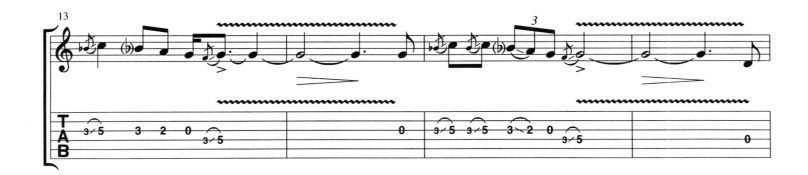

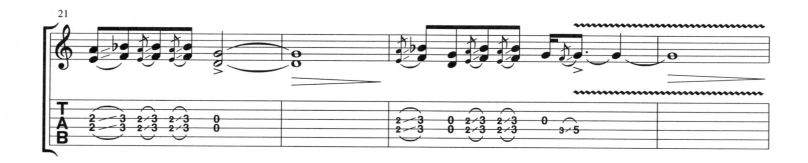

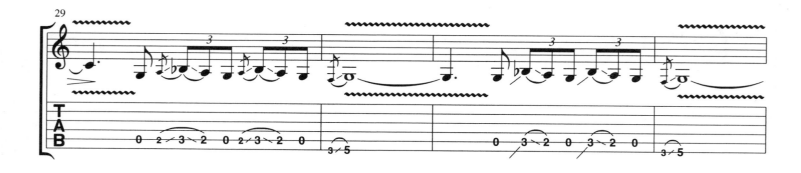

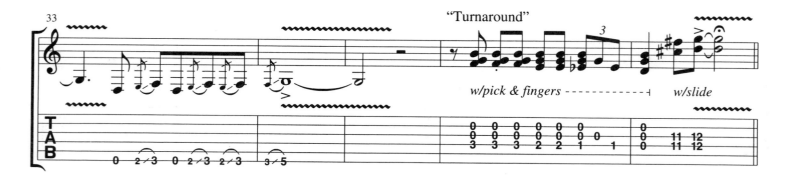

Anodized BigHeart
Anodized aluminum, with patented heart shaped design allows for a wide variety of tone colors.

BigHeart Violet Queen Bee
Satin anodized finish digs into the strings more than smooth glass slides providing a "rougher" sound.

BigHeart Resonator
Designed in conjunction with Dobro, reviewed best for electric guitar by Guitar Player magazine. The convex, concave and straight surfaces provide the widest variety of tone colors and control. The glazed porcelain finish produces a clean, brilliant and very loud tone without the harshness of metal slides.

BigHeart Boney Fingers
Polished porcelain, unglazed, great dynamics and wide variance of tone. One of the most versatile designs.

BigHeart Decorated Porcelain

BigHeart Coricidin Medicine Bottle
The traditional Coricidin medicine bottle slide with seamless glass. .

BigHeart Real Bottlenecks
Authentic recycled wine bottle bottleneck in the blues tradition.

BigHeart Porcelain
Dome-end glazed porcelain finish has a rich, clear sound. Domed top allows easy pin-pointing of notes.

BigHeart Handblown Glass
Dome-end glass slide. Hand blown glass provides the best and clearest highs. The dome-end allows easy pin-pointing of single note lines.

Marble Queen Bee
Traditional round design with flamed marble finish. Very smooth, like chromed steel.

Marble BigHeart
Heart shaped design with flamed marble finish. Very smooth, like chromed steel.

BEN HARPER

SECTION 5: PLAYIN' THE BLUES

A lot of territory has been covered exploring just one chord, as well as a number of phrases and techniques on the high end, and on the low end of the guitar, in open G tuning. But the most popular form of music in this style of guitar playing is called the **12-bar blues**. This means playing over changes, namely the I, IV and V chords. In the key of G that would be the G, C and D chords. The wonderful and easy thing about open tuning is that no matter which chord you play, you have all the notes necessary at one fret.

CD **(35)** *Example 21*

If you are in G, open string position, and want to go to the IV chord, C, you will see that the roots are located at the 5th fret of the 3rd and 5th strings. You can now transfer and play any phrase that you learned at the 12th fret to the 5th fret. You have all the same relationships based around the C chord that you had on the G chord. And the same theory applies to the D chord at the 7th fret. As long as you know where the IV and V chords are located by simply finding the root, you can build all those phrases together and play over a 12-bar blues.

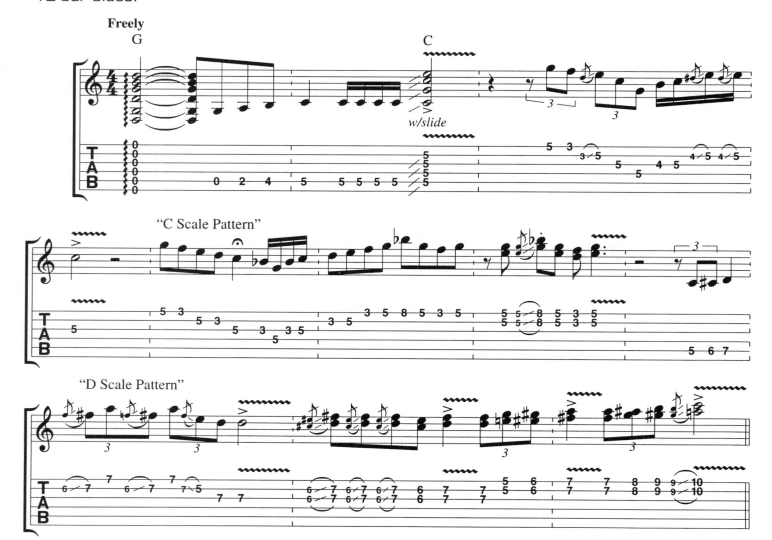

Example 22

Here is a 12-bar blues in open G tuning with accompaniment by a 2nd guitar in standard tuning. You can see how the same phrases, shapes and licks are used over each chord.

CD
(37) *Example 23*

There is another way to combine chord changes with open strings. This is referred to as the **"Muddy Waters"** style of slide guitar playing. This is an example of what he played in the 1940's. It is a self accompanied blues in open G tuning. There are different approaches to the IV and V chords here that are distinctly "Muddy Waters" traits. (See next example for details.)

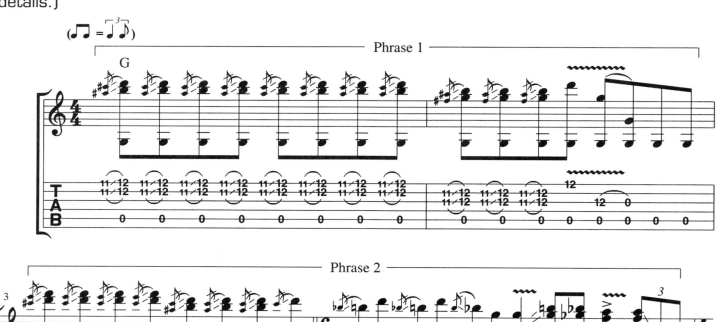

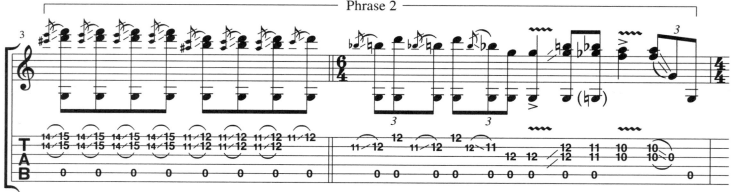

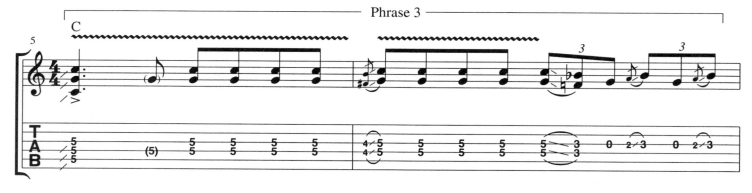

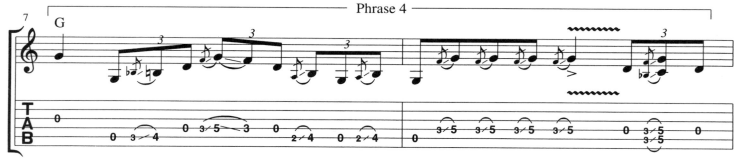

Example 24a

This is a detailed demonstration of the previous 12-bar, **self accompanied** blues. It is called "self accompaniment" because you play your own bass pattern under the melody. The bass, played with the pick, represents the root of the chord that you are playing over. You can also use a thumb pick, or your bare thumb to play the bass notes, while your fingers play the slide phrases. It can be tricky at first so practice slowly. Note the combination of slide and open strings over the IV and V chords. Measures 9 and 10 showcase Muddy Waters' trademark style by re-emphasizing an open string on a string below. The turnaround is a classic played by everyone who plays slide blues. Use only your fingers for bar 11 and use the slide again briefly in the 12th bar.

Example 24b

This is a slow treatment of Example 23 with a little different ending shown below.

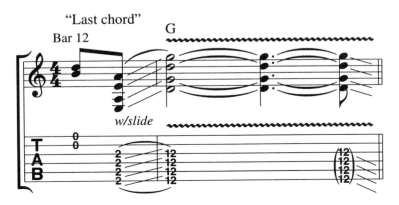

SECTION 6: THE CAPO

Slide players use a device called the **capo** to physically change the key that they are playing in. Even if you have tuned the guitar to open G, the capo, when placed on the neck, changes the pitch to suit, for example, the singer, who might be more comfortable singing in the new key. Capos come in all shapes and sizes and all accomplish the same thing. For example, when a capo is placed on the 2nd fret "key of G" fingerings will now sound in the key of A. When placed at the 3rd fret the same "key of G" fingerings will now sound in the key of B♭, etc.

Example 25

Suppose you wanted to change the key of the open G blues progression in Example 23 to the key of B♭. You would simply place the capo on the 3rd fret where the B♭ root on the 5th string is located. The capo acts as the "nut" would. All of your fingerings are now three frets higher and so the music "sounds" in B♭ although the fingerings are exactly the same as in the key of G. You can play everything you did before. Note: Tab numbers are counted from the capo. So a "2" in the tab is two frets above the capo.

JOHN HAMMOND JR.

SECTION 7: OPEN D TUNING

Open G tuning is probably the most popular tuning for country blues but there is another tuning that is used primarily by "city-blues" and electric guitar players — the open "D" tuning (D A D F♯ A D).

CD
(41) *Example 26a*

The open D tuning is simply an open E chord tuned down one whole step. The open strings should match the sound of the D chord, the 1st and 6th strings are lowered one whole step to "D," the 3rd string is brought down 1/2 step to F♯ and the 2nd string comes down one whole step to "A" (the 4th and 5th strings remain at "D" and "A". The main difference between the open G and the open D tuning is that the highest note, on the 1st string, is different in relation to the chord. In open G the 1st string represented the 5th of the chord whereas in open D the 1st string is the root. The melodies and phrases will have a different sound because of the different combinations of notes and as a result you will be able to play stronger melodies on the high strings.

↓⑥ = D ↓③ = F♯
⑤ = A ↓② = A
④ = D ↓① = D

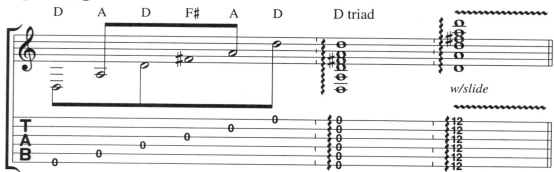

CD
(42) *Example 26b*

The 2nd, 3rd and 4th strings have the exact same relationship to each other that the top three strings had in open G tuning. The A, F♯ and D strings in open D (5th, 3rd & root) are in the same order as the D, B and G strings (5th 3rd & root) but down a string. So, you can play the same shapes you learned in open G tuning and extend the lines onto the 1st string.

finger pattern in "open D tuning"

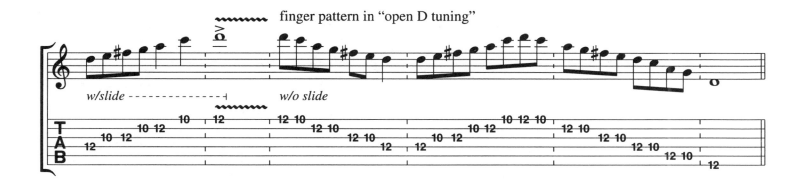

w/slide --------------- *w/o slide*

Example 27: Call and Response in Open D

To become familiar with the new patterns and phrases in open D tuning practice with this call and response exercise as you did earlier in the open G tuning.

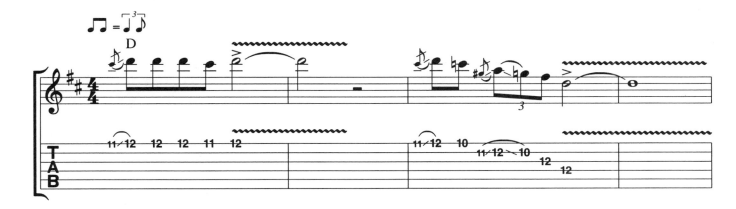

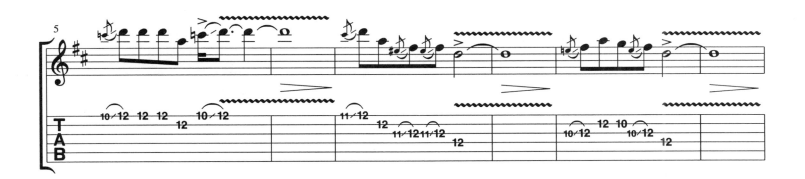

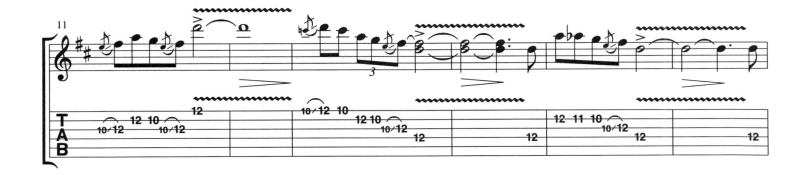

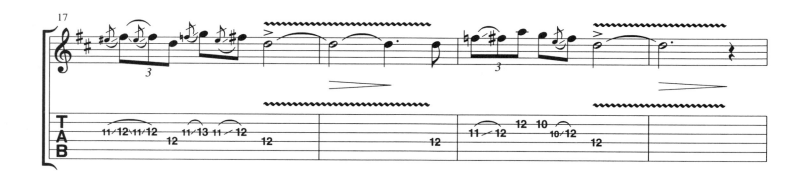

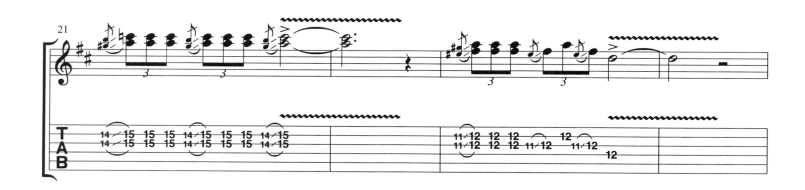

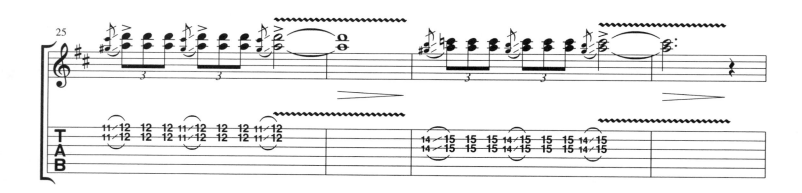

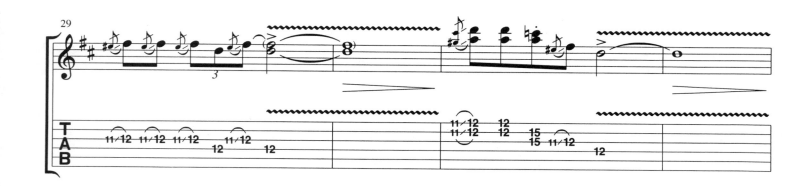

CD (44) *Example 28a*

Again, because of the similarities between the open G and the open D tunings you can use some of the same phrases, only moved over one string. What you played on the 3rd string in open G tuning can now be played on the 4th string of the open D tuning. Having the roots on the 1st and the 6th strings yields a much bigger sound and is quite an advantage.

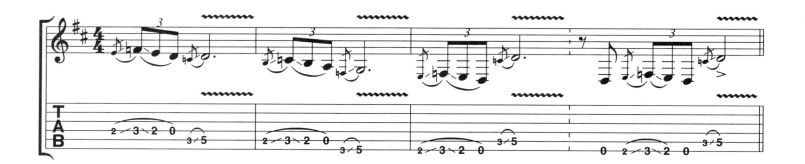

CD (45) *Example 28b*

The open D tuning has many possibilities on the 1st string as well.

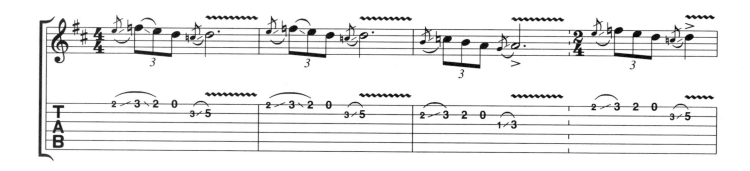

CD
46

Example 29

The descending notes in the "turnaround" phrase in the "Muddy Waters" blues in open G tuning were played on the 4th string. Now the descending notes are played on the 5th string against the open 4th string.

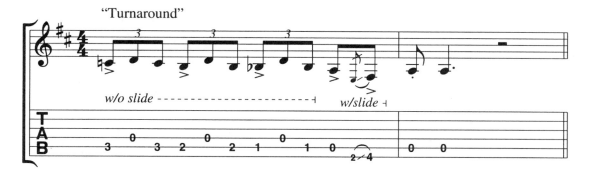

CD
47

Example 30a

The same rules apply to the open D tuning that were used in open G tuning. That is, when you use full chords, you can move the whole shape.

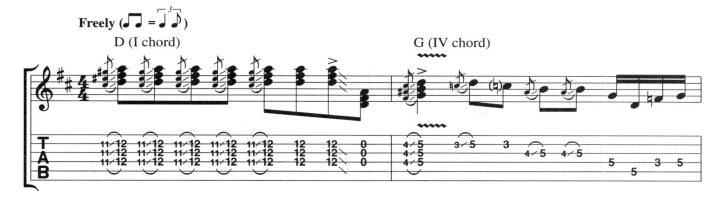

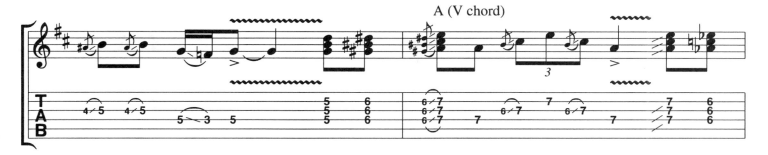

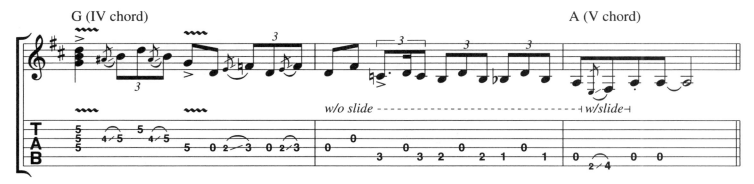

CD (48)

Example 30b

In Example 30a, the G chord (the IV of D) appeared in the 2nd measure. The root, G, is found on the 6th and 4th strings at the 5th fret. So, all the licks you played on the 12th fret can be played at the 5th fret. Likewise, for the V chord, A, all the same shapes apply again. That is the magic of open tuning. Learn one set of shapes and just move them around the neck, eliminating the need to map out the entire neck.

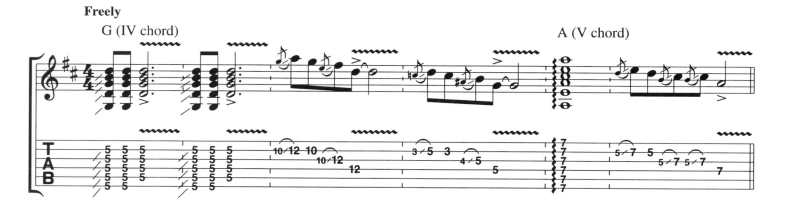

CD (49)

Example 31a: Elmore's Open D Blues

You may recognize this classic blues progression by **Elmore James**. It has been copied by virtually every blues slide player since the 1960's and it defines the open D tuning.

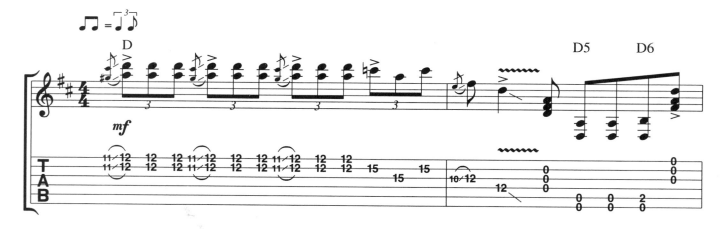

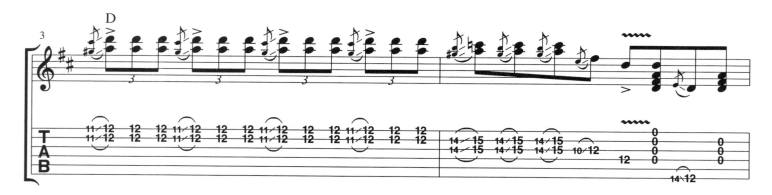

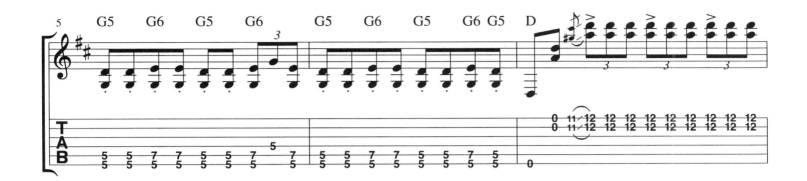

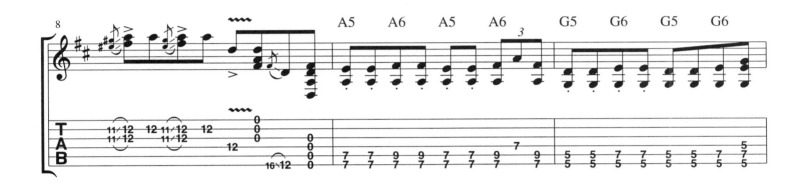

CD 50 *Example 31b*

This is a measure by measure breakdown of Example 31a. Most notable are the rhythmic figures in measures 2, 5, 6, 9 and 10 (See below). Play these shapes with an attitude and really "dig in" by using down strokes.

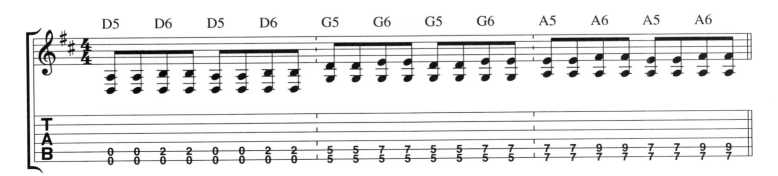

SECTION 8: STANDARD TUNING

CD 51 *Example 32a*

Although standard tuning is the tuning most guitarists use most of the time it is a bit tricky for slide; simply because there are not a lot of notes available on one fret that belong to the same chord. For example, to play the E chord at the 9th fret you would have to learn some new patterns. It is hard to intonate the 4th measure with a slide so a little re-fingering is in order. With the new fingering there is no need to move over two frets and you can slide easily into the last note.

CD 52 *Example 32b*

To play phrases in the key of E think of the shape of the chord and play around by ear to hear how, and which, notes fit the harmony. Play with the slide from measure four onward.

CD
(53) *Example 33*

Notice how you can play some characteristic slide phrases even in standard tuning. But because you are not tuned to a chord, as in open tuning, a problem surfaces in the 5th measure. It is difficult to dampen unwanted notes or even keep strings in tune with one another, especially with the slide.

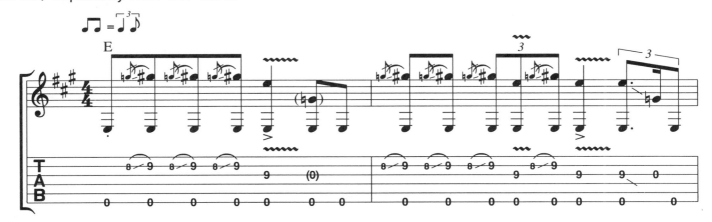

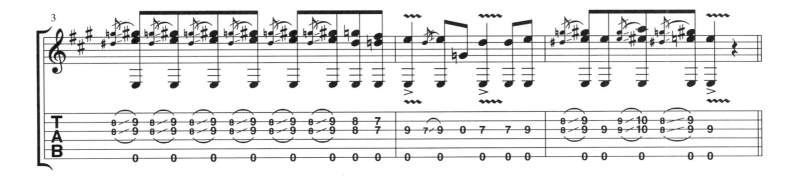

CD
(54) *Example 34*

Take some of the familiar phrases that you already play and duplicate them using a slide. This is a typical lick that most guitar players know, so try using a slide. You may have to re-finger certain passages or notes but it can be done. However, that is why most slide players use open tunings to simplify those relationships down to knowing only one pattern in each open tuning.

FINALE: PUTTING IT ALL TOGETHER

A lot of ground has been covered between the standard tuning, the basic technique of slide guitar, open G and open D tunings and all the variations. It is just the beginning and all this information may take a while to absorb. There is a lot to cover but most of the contents in this book you will learn with patience and careful listening. There are a wealth of slide recordings available. Once immersed in the discovery of new slide players try to emulate their basic sound and technique and make that an extension of your own individual sound.

Example 35

G BLUES

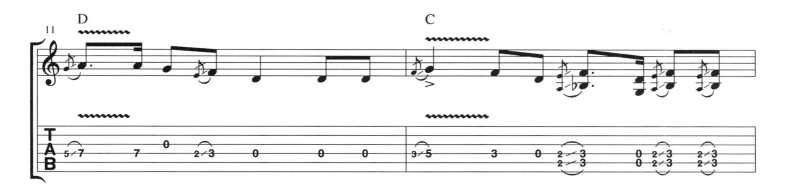

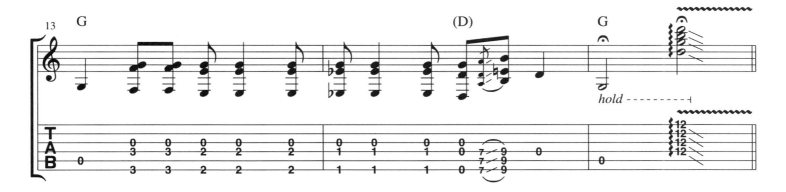

CD 57 Example 36

This outro tune is a "Muddy Waters Blues" in open G tuning. Enjoy!

MUDDY WATERS BLUES

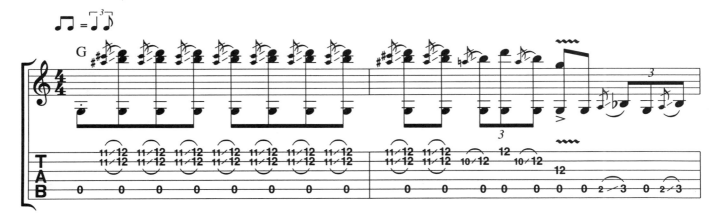

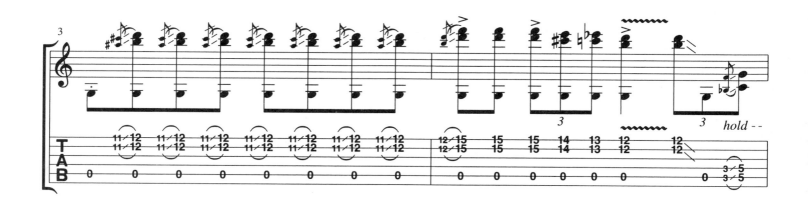

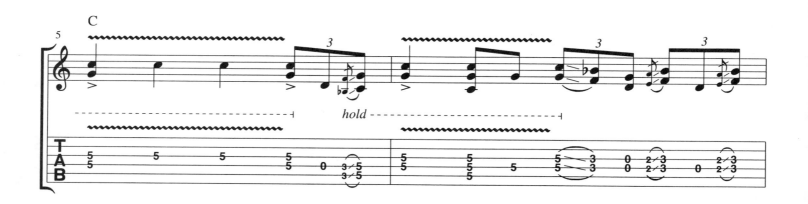

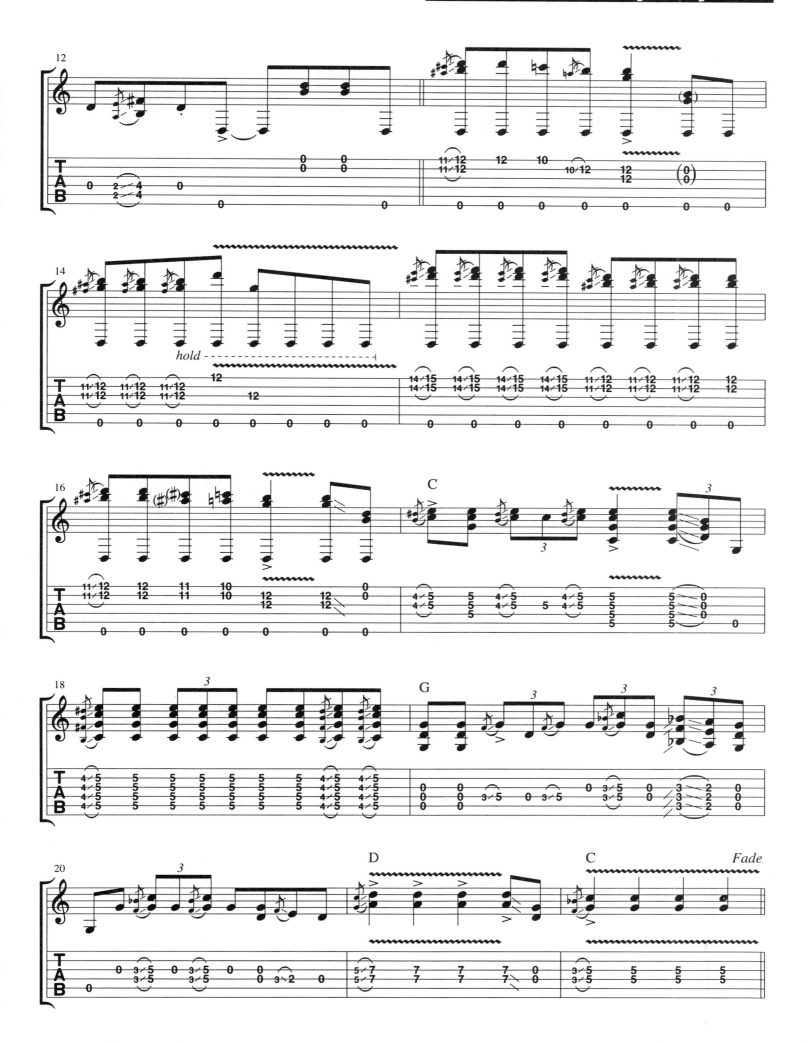

RHYTHM SLASHES

STRUM INDICATIONS: Strum with indicated rhythm.

The chord voicings are found on the first page of the transcription underneath the song title.

INDICATING SINGLE NOTES USING RHYTHM SLASHES: Very often single notes are incorporated into a rhythm part. The note name is indicated above the rhythm slash with a fret number and a string indication.

ARTICULATIONS

HAMMER ON: Play lower note, then "hammer on" to higher note with another finger. Only the first note is attacked.

LEFT HAND HAMMER: Hammer on the first note played on each string with the left hand.

PULL OFF: Play higher note, then "pull off" to lower note with another finger. Only the first note is attacked.

FRET-BOARD TAPPING: "Tap" onto the note indicated by + with a finger of the pick hand, then pull off to the following note held by the fret hand.

TAP SLIDE: Same as fretboard tapping, but the tapped note is slid randomly up the fretboard, then pulled off to the following note.

BEND AND TAP TECHNIQUE: Play note and bend to specified interval. While holding bend, tap onto note indicated.

LEGATO SLIDE: Play note and slide to the following note. (Only first note is attacked).

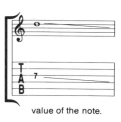

LONG GLISSAN-DO: Play note and slide in specified direction for the full value of the note.

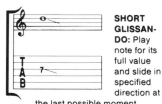

SHORT GLISSAN-DO: Play note for its full value and slide in specified direction at the last possible moment.

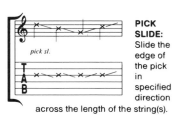

PICK SLIDE: Slide the edge of the pick in specified direction across the length of the string(s).

MUTED STRINGS: A percussive sound is made by laying the fret hand across all six strings while pick hand strikes specified area (low, mid, high strings).

PALM MUTE: The note or notes are muted by the palm of the pick hand by lightly touching the string(s) near the bridge.

TREMOLO PICKING: The note or notes are picked as fast as possible.

TRILL: Hammer on and pull off consecutively and as fast as possible between the original note and the grace note.

ACCENT: Notes or chords are to be played with added emphasis.

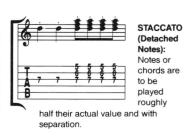

STACCATO (Detached Notes): Notes or chords are to be played roughly half their actual value and with separation.

DOWN STROKES AND UPSTROKES: Notes or chords are to be played with either a downstroke (⊓) or upstroke (∨) of the pick.

VIBRATO: The pitch of a note is varied by a rapid shaking of the fret hand finger, wrist, and forearm.

GUITAR TAB GLOSSARY **

TABLATURE EXPLANATION

READING TABLATURE: Tablature illustrates the six strings of the guitar. Notes and chords are indicated by the placement of fret numbers on a given string(s).

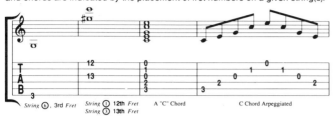

String ⑥, 3rd Fret   *String ① 12th Fret*   A "C" Chord   C Chord Arpeggiated
String ③ 13th Fret

BENDING NOTES

HALF STEP: Play the note and bend string one half step.*

PREBEND (Ghost Bend): Bend to the specified note, before the string is picked.

WHOLE STEP: Play the note and bend string one whole step.

PREBEND AND RELEASE: Bend the string, play it, then release to the original note.

WHOLE STEP AND A HALF: Play the note and bend string a whole step and a half.

REVERSE BEND: Play the already-bent string, then immediately drop it down to the fretted note.

SLIGHT BEND (Microtone): Play the note and bend string slightly to the equivalent of half a fret.

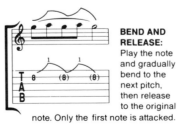

BEND AND RELEASE: Play the note and gradually bend to the next pitch, then release to the original note. Only the first note is attacked.

*A half step is the smallest interval in Western music; it is equal to one fret. A whole step equals two frets.

UNISON BEND: Play both notes and immediately bend the lower note to the same pitch as the higher note.

DOUBLE NOTE BEND: Play both notes and immediately bend both strings simultaneously.

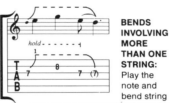

BENDS INVOLVING MORE THAN ONE STRING: Play the note and bend string while playing an additional note (or notes) on another string(s). Upon release, relieve pressure from additional note(s), causing original note to sound alone.

BENDS INVOLVING STATIONARY NOTES: Play notes and bend lower pitch, then hold until release begins (indicated at the point where line becomes solid).

TREMOLO BAR

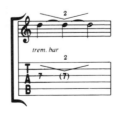

SPECIFIED INTERVAL: The pitch of a note or chord is lowered to a specified interval and then may or may not return to the original pitch. The activity of the tremolo bar is graphically represented by peaks and valleys.

UN-SPECIFIED INTERVAL: The pitch of a note or a chord is lowered to an unspecified interval.

HARMONICS

NATURAL HARMONIC: A finger of the fret hand lightly touches the note or notes indicated in the tab and is played by the pick hand.

ARTIFICIAL HARMONIC: The first tab number is fretted, then the pick hand produces the harmonic by using a finger to lightly touch the same string at the second tab number (in parenthesis) and is then picked by another finger.

ARTIFICIAL "PINCH" HAR-MONIC: A note is fretted as indicated by the tab, then the pick hand produces the harmonic by squeezing the pick firmly while using the tip of the index finger in the pick attack. If parenthesis are found around the fretted note, it does not sound. No parenthesis means both the fretted note and A.H. are heard simultaneously.

**By Kenn Chipkin and Aaron Stang

LEO KOTTKE